To Caleb, Joshua, and Noah
–P.Y.S.

For Doug
–R.C.

AUTHOR'S NOTE

I was four years old when most of this story takes place. It is based on my memories, as well as my sisters' and my father's, and on stories I have been told by others who were there. While I have tried to be as accurate as possible, I do not recall conversations word for word. Still, I do clearly remember their spirit, and have tried to capture it in these pages, along with a sense of the civil rights movement, as seen through the eyes of a young child.

ACKNOWLEDGMENTS

I am eternally grateful to my sisters, Andrea and Lisa, for sharing their stories with me; to Daddy, for raising me right and loving me always; to Jeffrey Goldberg, for giving me my big break; to Richard Abate, for taking a chance on me, and to Tina Wexler, for carrying the ball; to Anne Schwartz, for holding my hand and expertly guiding me through this whole process; to Raul Colón, for bringing this story to life so beautifully; and to my husband, Hilary, for his unparalleled love, support, and encouragement.

Text copyright © 2010 by Paula Young Shelton
Illustrations copyright © 2010 by Raul Colón

All rights reserved.
Published in the United States by
Schwartz & Wade Books,
an imprint of Random House Children's Books,
a division of Random House, Inc., New York.

Schwartz & Wade Books and the colophon
are trademarks of Random House, Inc.

Visit us on the Web!
www.randomhouse.com/kids

Educators and librarians, for a variety of teaching tools,
visit us at www.randomhouse.com/teachers

Library of Congress Cataloging-in-Publication Data
Shelton, Paula Young.
Child of the civil rights movement / Paula Young Shelton ;
illustrated by Raul Colón. – 1st ed.
p. cm.
ISBN 978-0-375-84314-3 (trade)
ISBN 978-0-375-95414-6 (glb)
1. Shelton, Paula Young–Juvenile literature. 2. Selma to
Montgomery Rights March (1965 : Selma, Ala.)–Juvenile
literature. 3. Civil rights movements–Alabama–Selma–
History–20th century–Juvenile literature. 4. African
Americans–Civil rights–Alabama–Selma–History–
20th century–Juvenile literature. 5. Selma (Ala.)–
Race relations–History–20th century–Juvenile literature.
I. Colón, Raul. II. Title.
F334.S4S54 2010
323.1196'073076147–dc22
2008045855

The text of this book is set in Aged.
The illustrations were created by laying a wash on watercolor paper using Winsor & Newton Aureolin Yellow.
The final images were drawn in lead pencil, followed by numerous washes in sepias and browns.
Layers of colored pencil were added, and the images were finished with black lithograph pencil.

MANUFACTURED IN MALAYSIA

3 5 7 9 10 8 6 4 2

First Edition

Child of the Civil Rights Movement

by Paula Young Shelton

illustrated by Raul Colón

schwartz & wade books · new york

Going Home

Mama was from Alabama,
Daddy was from Louisiana—
the Deep South.
They had been called bad names,
treated badly,
told, "You can't do that!"
just because of the color of their skin.

They grew up with Jim Crow—
laws that said black people had to sit in
the back of the bus,
the last car of the train,
the balcony of the movie theater.
Laws that said black people couldn't vote.

I was born in New York, where there was no Jim Crow.
But one day when Mama and Daddy were watching the news,
they saw something called the Freedom Riders–
black and white students riding buses together
from the North to the South
to protest the bad laws.
They watched as racists pulled the students from their seats
and set the buses on fire.
"We have to go help!" my father exclaimed.
"We have to go home," my mother declared.

So Mama and Daddy packed up
their three little girls—
Andrea, Lisa, and me—
and we went back to Georgia,
back to Jim Crow,
where whites could
but blacks could not.
Back to the heart of the civil rights movement.

My First Protest

In our new home in Atlanta,
Jim Crow was everywhere.
At first, I thought Jim Crow was a big black crow
that squawked whenever a black person
tried to get a good seat.
"CAWWW, CAWWW, you can't sit there!"

But really, he was a white man
who lived long ago.
He painted his face black
and made fun of African Americans.
He didn't sound very nice to me.
I guess that's why they named the laws after him,
because they weren't very nice either.

Despite Jim Crow, a few restaurants had opened
where blacks and whites could eat together.
One Sunday Mama and Daddy decided to see
how far things had really come.
So after church we went to have brunch
at the brand-new Holiday Inn restaurant.

We stepped into the fancy lobby
with chandeliers hanging from the ceiling,
and we asked for a table.
But they wouldn't let us in.

We looked at all the empty tables
with white tablecloths
and the few white faces that stared at us
in horror.
All we wanted was to sit down and eat.
I was so hungry that I started crying.
But they wouldn't let us in.

"My baby's hungry," Mama said
while I kept crying, louder and louder.
Mama and Daddy didn't try to stop me;
they simply sat me down and let me cry.
And did I ever!
I screamed at the top of my lungs,
my very first protest, my own little sit-in.
But still they wouldn't let us in.

Uncle Martin

Uncle Martin had a big, broad smile
and eyes that twinkled.
"Come here, girl," he'd say
whenever our families would meet
at one of the only pools for African Americans
in Atlanta, the Ollie Street YMCA.
"Are you ready to get in that water
and teach me how to swim?"

Run!
I would run as fast
as my skinny little legs could carry me.
Run and leap!
Leap into his wide-open arms and fly!
Fly as he threw me high into the air.
"Nooooo!" I would scream, and laugh,
my arms clasped tightly around his neck
as he pretended to throw me in.

But Uncle Martin wasn't really my uncle—
not by blood, anyway.
We were close because our fathers
worked together.
Close because our mothers worried together.
Close because we all struggled together.
Close because we were brought together
for a common goal,
a common good.
We were one family—
the family of the American civil rights movement.

The Civil Rights Family

Like all families, we'd have dinner together, and
since there were so few restaurants that served African Americans,
we'd often eat at friends' houses.
We might walk around the corner to Uncle Ralph and Aunt Juanita's,
or go to Uncle Martin and Aunt Coretta's,
or everyone would come to our house.

One night when it was our turn to host,
I sat under the kitchen table,
watching and listening—
watching the folks in the dining room,
listening to the booming voices,
angry sometimes,
sometimes very angry.
They were talking about Selma, Alabama,
where, as in most cities in the South,
blacks had been denied the right to vote.
They were organizing a huge march to protest—
from Selma to Montgomery.
They had already marched twice before.
And twice before they'd been beaten back.

RANDOLPH BLACKWELL

HOSEA WILLIAMS

ANDREW YOUNG

JAMES ORANGE

With everyone trying to talk at once,
I thought they sounded just like
instruments tuning up before a concert.
Blackwell, the professor,
was like a trombone,
soooooo smooth,
clearly presenting the facts.
Hosea ambled around the table in his overalls,
tooting like a tuba.
"I was in Selma last time,
and we've got to go back."
"Let's wait," Daddy said,
the mellow saxophone of reason.
I flinched when Big Orange stood up,
his huge frame towering
above everyone else.
"That ain't right, Andy,"
he boomed like a bass drum.
"We got to go help these folks *now!*"

Uncle Ralph agreed,
his voice rising melodically
above the horns and drum
like a violin.
Then Aunt Dorothy's sweet soprano
joined in.
"We've got to get the young people involved,"
she sang.
"If they can go to Vietnam to fight,
they can fight at home."
Mama's flute chimed in from the kitchen,
reminding the men that the women
would be the key to any march's success.

Meanwhile, Uncle Martin sat silent
and listened to the orchestra play.

RALPH ABERNATHY

DOROTHY COTTON

JEAN CHILDS YOUNG

MARTIN LUTHER KING, JR.

Uncle Martin loved the music of his friends and
knew that each instrument needed to be heard.
But he also knew that in the end
they must come together like a symphony,
as one.

"Paula baby," Mama said, "set the table."
I slipped out from my hiding place,
grabbed the napkins and forks,
and bounced into the dining room,
my nightgown fluttering behind me.

The discussion continued as passionately as before,
but as I set each place, the person seated paused,
looked at me and smiled,
patted my head, or gave me a gentle hug.

"Dinner's ready," Mama called,
carrying in a large dish of macaroni and cheese.
"Let me help you, Jean,"
Aunt Dorothy volunteered,
and went to get the bowl of green beans
and a pitcher of sweet tea.
In the kitchen,
Andrea grabbed the baked chicken
and marched in first, as always.
Lisa came next,
carrying a big, beautiful salad,
and I got the basket of corn bread.

Some time later, when everyone was done,
there were hugs and kisses
and "I'm so full I can't walk's"
and raving about the macaroni and cheese,
which seemed to come from a magic pot
that filled up every time you scooped some
of the creamy casserole onto a plate.
No matter how many people came to dinner,
there was always enough to go around,
enough to strengthen,
enough to comfort
the family of the civil rights movement.

Selma to Montgomery

Daddy was away a lot—
Alabama,
Mississippi,
Florida,
Georgia—
while Mama stayed home to care for us.
He was away marching,
organizing,
registering voters,
protesting unfair laws,
teaching nonviolence.
Sometimes he was beaten.
Sometimes he went to jail for breaking the Jim Crow laws
that said blacks and whites couldn't eat together,
or go to school together,
or even drink from the same water fountain.
Sometimes he went to jail just for marching.

But when Daddy was getting ready to march to Montgomery,
Mama said, "I'm marching too."
So they packed up their three little girls
and we headed to Selma.

We gathered at Brown Chapel AME Church the next morning
with thousands of others.

I looked around and saw so many different kinds of people.

Black and white.

Young and old.

Rich and poor.

There were Jewish rabbis, Catholic priests,

and lots and lots of Baptist ministers.

There was even a man with one leg

who everybody called Sunshine.

There were people from the South
and people from the North.
One group had come all the way from Hawaii,
and they handed out leis to the leaders.
Excitement flashed through the air like lightning.
Then Uncle Martin linked arms with a priest
and extended his hand to Aunt Coretta
as if to ask her to dance.
And the march was on.

Since I was only four years old, I could walk for just a little while.

Mama carried me until she got tired,

and then I got passed from aunt to uncle to aunt.

Lisa was eight, still small enough to ride on Daddy's shoulders

as he jogged up and down the long line of marchers,

shouting at us to pick up the pace

or starting a song to keep our spirits high.

He ran up and down that long line so many times,

he said he marched from Selma to Montgomery

ten times that week!

Andrea was ten years old and she marched proudly that day.

"Do you want to ride?" Mama asked,

offering to put her in one of the cars that followed behind

for old folks and young folks and just plain tired folks.

"No, I want to march," she answered firmly.

That night I fell asleep in Mama's arms.

When I woke up, I was at my grandparents' house,

not far from Selma.

Andrea, Lisa, and I spent

the rest of the week there while

Mama and Daddy continued on.

It would take four days to march the fifty miles
from Selma to Montgomery,
the National Guard escorting the peaceful protesters
the whole way, to keep them safe.
All over the country, people watched on TV
as the group marched triumphantly into Montgomery.
President Johnson saw it too.

The Voting Rights Act of 1965

Then one joyous evening, the sixth of August, 1965,
my family sat around our small black-and-white television set.
Uncle Martin stood over the shoulder of President Johnson
and watched him sign the bill
that would make sure *all* people—
black and white—
could vote
and no one could stop them.

Curled up on Mama's lap, I thought about our march
while pictures flashed across the screen.
Andrea and Lisa shouted at the TV,
pointing out folks we knew
and the places we'd been.
We talked about the singing, the praying,
the friends and family,
even the tired feet.
It made me glow with pride to know
that I had played one small part.
But even then I also knew
that we'd won just one battle
and there were many more to come.

And one day,
when Mama and Daddy were too tired to march,
too weary to carry us on their shoulders,
too exhausted to fight another battle,
the baton would pass to us
and we would march on—
children of the civil rights movement.

MORE ABOUT THE PEOPLE IN THIS BOOK

ANDREW YOUNG (born 1932), my daddy, was a young minister with the National Council of Churches when he and my mama, JEAN CHILDS YOUNG (1933–1994), got the "calling" to help my uncle Martin shape the American civil rights movement. Daddy began training people in nonviolent social action and later became vice president of the SCLC (the Southern Christian Leadership Conference), which fought for civil rights through nonviolence. Mama taught school and took care of the children. Daddy was elected to Congress and, later, became mayor of Atlanta, while Mama served as first lady and helped start a junior college. President Jimmy Carter appointed Daddy U.S. ambassador to the United Nations and made Mama chair of the International Year of the Child. Daddy and Mama raised four children: Andrea, Lisa, me, and Bo. Daddy now runs a business called GoodWorks that helps develop businesses and communities in Africa.

MARTIN LUTHER KING, JR. (1929–1968), was a Baptist minister with a great desire to help his fellow human being and an amazing speaker who inspired millions. Being chosen to lead the Montgomery bus boycott launched his career as leader of the American civil rights movement. He led protest marches, wrote books, gave speeches, was beaten, and went to jail, but he never showed hatred. He was a loving father and a devoted husband to CORETTA SCOTT KING (1927–2006), who was a student of music when they met. Though never able to pursue her musical career, she helped raise money for and awareness of the cause. After her husband's death, she campaigned to establish Martin Luther King Day. She and Uncle Martin had four children: Yolanda, Martin III, Dexter, and Bernice, who have all worked to realize their father's dream.

RALPH ABERNATHY (1926–1990) was a Baptist minister and Uncle Martin's closest friend. Together they helped organize the Montgomery bus boycott and cofounded the MIA (Montgomery Improvement Association) and the SCLC. Later, Uncle Ralph became president of the SCLC and organized the Poor People's Campaign to bring attention to the problems of America's homeless and hungry.

RANDOLPH BLACKWELL (1927–1981), known to his friends simply as Blackwell, was a lawyer, a professor, and an organizer—a Renaissance man who loved classical music. At fourteen, he joined the NAACP (National Association for the Advancement of Colored People), and he continued to fight for civil rights for the rest of his life. He served as a field director of the Voter Education Program, working to register voters; as director of Southern Rural Action, an organization committed to helping poor communities; and as program director of the SCLC.

DOROTHY COTTON (born 1930) was the highest-ranking woman in the SCLC as its education director and worked to train people in nonviolent social action. A gifted speaker, storyteller, and singer, she served as vice president for field operations for the King Center and has devoted her life to creating a more humane world.

JAMES ORANGE (1942–2008), known as Big Orange because he was so big and tall, was a high school football star when he began working with Uncle Martin to recruit fellow students in Birmingham, Alabama. His ability to motivate others made Big Orange one of the most effective field organizers of the civil rights movement, and he later applied his skills to the labor movement with the AFL-CIO.

HOSEA WILLIAMS (1926–2000) was returning from World War II, during which he earned a Purple Heart, when he was beaten and arrested for drinking from a "white only" water fountain in a bus station. It was then that he decided God had spared his life so that he could fight racism, which he did from then on. He began working with the NAACP and later joined the SCLC, in which he held several positions. He was active in Georgia politics and founded Hosea Feed the Hungry, which still provides hot meals and other free services in Atlanta for those in need.

BIBLIOGRAPHY

Academy of Achievement, biography of Coretta Scott King, copyright 1996–2009, American Academy of Achievement: www.achievement.org/autodoc/page/kin1bio-1

Civil Rights Digital Library, article on Dorothy Cotton, copyright 2009 Digital Library of Georgia: http://crdl.usg.edu/people/c/cotton_dorothy_1930/

Dorothy Cotton Web site: www.dorothycotton.com/html/biography.html

Markiewicz, David. "The Rev. James Orange, civil rights activist, dies at 65: Atlanta resident was 'one of the great figures in the movement,' *The Atlanta Journal-Constitution,* published February 16, 2008, copyright 2009 *The Atlanta Journal-Constitution*: www.ajc.com/metro/content/metro/obits/stories/2008/02/16/orange_0217.html

New Georgia Encyclopedia, History & Archaeology, article on Hosea Williams, copyright 2004–2009 by the Georgia Humanities Council and the University of Georgia Press: www.georgiaencyclopedia.org/nge/Article.jsp?id=h-2721&hl=y

New Georgia Encyclopedia, History & Archaeology, article on Ralph Abernathy, copyright 2004–2009 by the Georgia Humanities Council and the University of Georgia Press: www.georgiaencyclopedia.org/nge/Article.jsp?id=h-2736&hl=y

Young, Andrew. *An Easy Burden: The Civil Rights Movement and the Transformation of America.* New York: HarperCollins, 1996.

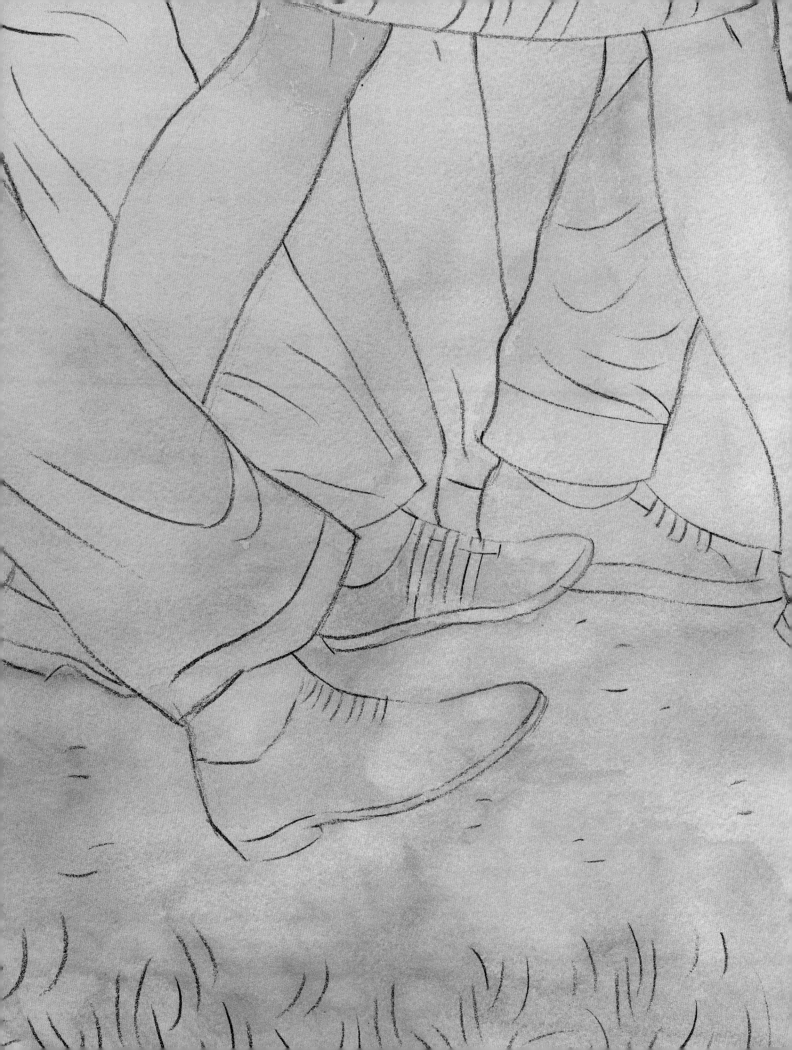